THEY DIED TOO YOUNG

CHRIS FARLEY

Marilyn Anderson

CHELSEA HOUSE PUBLISHERS
Philadelphia

The Chelsea House World Wide Web address is
http://www.chelseahouse.com

Printed and bound in The Hashemite Kingdom of Jordan.
First Printing
1 3 5 7 9 8 6 4 2

Cover photo: Chris Farley (NBC-TV)

Library of Congress Cataloging-in-Publication Data
Anderson, Marilyn D.
    Chris Farley / Marilyn Anderson.
        p. cm. — (They died too young.)
    Including bibliographical references and index.
    Summary: A biography of the comedian who got his start on
"Saturday Night Live" and starred in such movies as "Tommy Boy"
and "Beverly Hills Ninja," before dying of a drug overdose.
    ISBN 0-7910-5860-3
    1. Farley, Chris, 1964–1997—Juvenile literature.   2. Comedians—
United States—Biography—Juvenile literature.   3. Actors—United
States—Biography—Juvenile literature.   [1. Farley, Chris, 1964–1997.
2. Comedians.   3. Actors and actresses.]   I. Title.   II. Series.
PN2287.F33 A85 2000
792.7'028'092--dc21
[B]   00-027711
                                                           CIP

Picture Credits: AP Photo: pp. 4, 8, 10, 20, 24, 28, 35, 42; Paramount
Pictures: pp. 30, 33, 36; Reuters/Archive Photos: pp. 16, 39; Universal
Pictures: p. 22

Publishing Coordinator Jim McAvoy
Editorial Assistant Rob Quinn
Contributing Editor Amy Handy

The author wishes to thank Michael Price, Pat Finn, Mike Shoemaker,
and *Madison* magazine for their help in preparing this book.

ABOUT THE AUTHOR

Marilyn Anderson grew up on a dairy farm in Minnesota. After college she
taught K–12 music for 17 years in Minnesota, Vermont, and Indiana. Her first
nonfiction book was published in 1983. Sixteen children's chapter books
followed, including her series about Barkley (a dog), *The Bubble Gum Monster*
books, and *The Horse That Came to Breakfast*. She also writes stories and arti-
cles for magazines, is a published playwright, and teaches writing to adults. In
her spare time, she trains and shows dressage horses and serves as substitute
organist at her church. Mrs. Anderson and her husband live in Bedford, Indiana.

CONTENTS

Chris Farley and Chris Rock (left) attend a 1990 press conference, where it was announced that they would be joining the cast of *Saturday Night Live*.

HITTING THE BIG TIME

On October 27, 1990, a 26-year-old comedian named Christopher Crosby Farley waited backstage at a major television studio. He was so scared and primed to perform that he could hardly keep his huge body from exploding into action.

He was about to be featured in a scene with a big Hollywood star on a show seen coast to coast. Chris Farley was in New York City and was about to appear on *Saturday Night Live*.

Since its beginning back in 1975, *Saturday Night Live* (or *SNL*) has served as a launching ground for many famous personalities. The extraordinary talents of stars such as Steve Martin, Eddie Murphy, Julia Louis-Dreyfus, Bill Murray, Billy Crystal, Chevy Chase, Dan Aykroyd, John Candy, and John Belushi were first seen and then developed on this raunchy, cutting-edge TV show.

Actually, Belushi was one of the big reasons Chris was there that night. When Chris was much younger, he and his dad had gone to the movie *National Lampoon's Animal House* and loved it. Seeing the way his dad laughed uncontrollably at the overweight Belushi's antics made a big impression on Chris. He began to think of a career in comedy for himself.

Now, after several years of performing for live audiences in Wisconsin and Illinois, this would be Chris's first major TV performance. Chris knew that he was funny, and he'd had small parts before on *SNL*. This time, however, he had a big part opposite Patrick Swayze, who had recently starred in the wildly successful movie *Ghost*.

The pressure on Chris was intense because *SNL* is, as the title says, live, meaning mistakes are beamed directly to the entire country. His performance would likely classify him as the newest comedy sensation or as a "jerk."

Chris was still new to *SNL* and to New York. Only a few months earlier, *SNL*'s creator Lorne Michaels had seen Chris working at Chicago's Second City Theatre and been impressed enough to hire Chris for his popular TV show.

Awestruck on his first day of work in New York, Chris, the shaggy-haired Midwesterner, had met a slim, well-groomed Arizona native named David Spade, who wrote for *SNL*. They walked to the NBC studios together. By the time they got to work, they were already laughing uproariously and on the way to a long-term friendship.

Actually entering the 17th floor of 30 Rockerfeller Center, where *SNL* is filmed each week, and joining the sophisticated New Yorkers who put *Saturday Night Live* on the air was a humbling experience for Chris. This was where some of the kings of comedy had worked. He was sure he stuck out like a sore thumb.

A lot of people think that *Saturday Night Live* is mostly improvised—made up as it goes along. But *SNL* is only supposed to *seem* like improvisation. The show Chris was about to be part of had begun to take shape six days earlier, when he and the rest of cast had been introduced to Patrick Swayze, the guest host for the week. Chris had been practically speechless when he first came face to face with the star.

That was Monday, and on Tuesday Chris was told to come up with some ideas for possible sketches. Chris did his best, but he had to admit, "I'm not much of a writer."

On Wednesday the entire *SNL* family gathered in a conference room. Writers and performers arrived in blue jeans and sweatshirts and sat down at a big oval table to present their ideas. The atmosphere was friendly but competitive.

About 40 rough sketches were proposed, and writer Robert Smigel suggested that Chris use his huge, round body for laughs in a dance number with handsome lady's man Swayze.

The show's producers considered the idea. They had seen Chris dance before, and they knew he was good. He'd done well earlier in a small part in a parody of the popular television show *Twin Peaks* and been a hilarious drunk the week New York Yankee owner George Steinbrenner was guest host. They decided it was time to let Chris break through. The sketch was one of the 10 chosen to be developed for use on that week's show.

Chris loved the sketch proposal, and when he got his script, he immediately began to study his lines. He considered the moves he'd make to bring his character "Barney" to life. Meanwhile, he hoped that his sketch would not be one of the two or three routinely cut on Saturdays to meet the show's 90-minute format.

On Thursday Chris and Swayze bounced their lines off each other and worked on the sexy dance they would do together. The rest of the cast cracked up when Chris, with all his excess poundage, pranced around next to the fit-and-trim Swayze. On Friday the performers and the camera men worked on placement of the performers. The sketch was looking good.

Saturday was devoted to final preparations for the show, and at 8:00 P.M. the cast started dress rehearsal. Chris struggled into the elegant sleeveless white shirt and tight black pants that he would wear for his all-important sketch with Swayze. Then he began to sweat.

Dress rehearsal went great. The more he and Patrick danced, the more Chris hammed it up. The wilder he got, the more those watching laughed. Chris was in heaven. He loved making people laugh. He could hardly believe he was getting paid for doing the same kind of stuff that used to get him into trouble back in school.

When the rehearsal was over, Chris and the rest of the cast met in Lorne Michaels's office to hear which sketches had been cut and what might be added. To Chris's relief, his spot with Swayze was still in, but the tension from then until airtime never let up. New bits were added or subtracted right up until they went in front of the cameras.

The band tuned up, and suddenly the show was on the

Chris Farley and Molly Shannon perform a skit on *Saturday Night Live* that originally aired October 25, 1997.

air. Part of the cast did a square dance sketch that led into the famous intro, "Live from New York, it's Saturday night!" After some opening camera shots of various New York City sights, Swayze did an elegant balloom dance with his wife. Chris kept on sweating.

Hans and Frans, two fake German bodybuilders in inflated suits, did a bit in which they admired Swayze's flexibility. There were phony commercials, then a sketch that was a takeoff on *Ghost*. Chris moved around and tried to stay loose.

Singer Mariah Carey performed "Vision of Love," leading into a station break. Then, as the goofy news sketch "Weekend Update" played, the director called for Chris.

He hurried to stand next to Swayze on a small stage in

8   *They Died Too Young*

front of a sign reading "Chippendales." They wished each other luck. The director started the countdown: ". . . three, two, one . . ." He pointed at Chris and Swayze. They were on!

The camera moved back to reveal three people sitting at a table ready to judge the men on their dance moves. One judge told the characters played by Chris and Swayze that, after five hours of auditioning, this was to be the final tryout. What they did here would determine who would join "The Chippendales." The audience knew that the Chippendales are a troop of male strippers famous for dance routines that make women drool.

Chris and Patrick looked at each other and seemed properly impressed. Their hands fluttered around. They giggled. Then the music began to throb, and they began to move. Chris was incredibly graceful for a man his size. They twisted and gyrated and showed off their wonderful hard bodies, but of course, Chris didn't have a hard body. He looked ridiculous trying to be a sex symbol.

When they both pulled off their shirts to show even more, Chris's rolls of flab hung over the belt of his tight pants and took on a life of their own.

The studio audience went wild. Finally the music stopped, and the "judges" were very kind. They told Chris that they were sorry, but Patrick was the new Chippendale dancer. (Big surprise.) The skit finished with Chris and Patrick congratulating each other on how great each had been and vowing to be buds forever. It was a classic performance.

When the show was over, Chris was flying high as he joined the rest of the cast for the traditional sign-off at the end of the broadcast. Other performers patted him on the back and congratulated him on his big moment. Chris nodded and smiled, remembering the studio audience's laughter. At that moment, all he wanted out of life was more of the same.

As a child, Chris often used humor to deflect
teasing about his weight.

"I WANT TO BE A STAND-UP COMEDIAN"

Chris's mother says he was born big. She declares that when he entered the world on February 15, 1964, he weighed a whopping 12 pounds, 11 ounces!

His father, Tom Sr., another very heavy guy, owned an asphalt-paving company. Chris was the middle child of five, with three brothers (Tom Jr., John, and Kevin) and one sister (Barbara). Their close-knit Irish-American family lived in Maple Bluff, one of the nicer sections of Madison, Wisconsin.

Chris was raised Catholic, and his early faith in God stuck with him. No matter how outrageous his life got later on, he tried to get to mass.

Suppers at the Farley home were a riot, with seven funny people clowning around and inventing "in-jokes." Many of those jokes showed up in Chris's routines later on, and brother Tom says that sometimes he was the only person laughing like crazy when Chris slipped in a family one-liner.

Chris was funny at Edgewood Grade School, too, so funny that one day his mother had to go meet with Sisters Claris and Angelica. His mother was told that "the children at school are laughing at Christopher, not with him," though that may or may not have been the case.

A roly-poly guy even then, Chris was popular, but he also took lots of teasing. Kids called him names like Fartly, Tubby, and Fatso. On bad days he would go home after school and head straight to the basement to watch *Gilligan's Island* and eat a gallon of ice cream. No wonder he tried so hard for laughs. It got him attention. It helped him make friends. It made him feel special.

Summers were spent at a Boy Scout camp in Woodruff,

Wisconsin, where Chris went on long canoe trips and got into some trouble. Once he cut all the ropes on the ropes course, and other Scouts fell in the mud. He was also famous for his "mooning."

At camp he also got some of his first stage experience. Richard Wenzel, who was in charge of the little shows the boys put on, coached Chris on stage presence and on how to time his jokes for the biggest laughs.

In spite of being heavy, Chris was very athletic. His brother Tom recalled, "As a 10-year-old, [Chris would] hit the water with those big, broad shoulders of his and leave those other kids in the dust."

He was good at other sports, too, especially football, and was named all-city defensive lineman in his senior year. But when he was younger and didn't play much, Chris hated just sitting on the bench in his clean uniform. Sometimes he'd lie down and roll in the dirt to make it look as if he'd played.

Friends remember he had a compulsion to touch the ground twice before the snap of every ball. Chris thought about becoming a pro, but he eventually realized that even at 5 feet, 9 inches tall and 230 pounds, he still wasn't big enough for that.

"A nun's nightmare" was how he described his high school years. "Once someone dared me to grab a fire extinguisher and spray it all over study hall," he told a reporter from *Playboy* magazine. "I sprayed everyone in study hall, plus the windows and the nun. But I got out of it because . . . you could bamboozle [the nuns]. . . . 'Sister, I saw smoke. I swear I wanted to help out,' and she believed me."

Another friend dared him to streak through the halls, and of course Chris did it. He got to the end of the hall and started back only to run right into one of the nuns and knock her over. He couldn't talk his way out of that one.

Other guys thought Chris's antics were amusing, but crazy characters who look like the Pillsbury Dough Boy don't necessarily attract girls. Not having a girlfriend bothered him.

When Chris graduated from high school in 1982, his teachers no doubt sighed with relief to see him leave for Marquette University in Milwaukee. Chris's dad wanted him to major in business administration and take over the family paving company, so Chris obediently signed up for courses in business. But his heart wasn't in them.

About halfway through Chris's sophomore year, he stopped in at Associate Dean Michael Price's office to see what classes were required the next semester. Chris told Price that he was thinking about dropping out of college.

"Oh?" said Price. "And what did you think you were going to do then?"

"I'd like to be a stand-up comedian," said Chris.

"Oh," said Price.

Chris was surprised that the dean had taken this news so calmly. "You're not going to laugh?"

The dean assured Chris that he wasn't but warned that a life in show business can be rough.

Chris said he knew that, but he still wanted to try being a comedian. His biggest worry was how to convince his parents to give him a chance. "They'll say 'it's a big risk. It's a rough life. You won't have a home base. There's no security. No benefit package.'" Price told Chris to write down those negatives, prepare his arguments, and that Price would arrange a conference with Mr. and Mrs. Farley.

At the meeting, Chris went over his list of negatives and talked about each. Chris's dad was very impressed with how much his son had thought about his decision, but the senior Farley still hoped Chris would change his mind and take over the company his grandfather had started.

Finally a compromise was reached. Chris would change his major from business to interpersonal communications. This would free him from the math classes he hated and let him concentrate on skills of persuasion and communication.

Next, Price convinced Chris to minor in theater and to get involved in Marquette's drama department. Chris tried out for the next play that came along, a modern work by Sam Shephard called *The Curse of the Starving Class*. It was definitely not a comedy. Chris played the part of a policeman and proved that he could act.

Now that he was free to dream of a career in comedy, Chris blossomed. He enjoyed his classes in acting, dancing, writing, religion, and philosophy. He was in other plays and was on the rugby team, which was almost like a family. He was good friends with the assistant rugby coach, Jesuit priest Matt Foley, but his best friend was a fellow player named Pat Finn.

When Chris and Pat were in the same class, craziness was sure to follow. In speech class, for example, they were supposed to give orations about summer jobs they had held. About noon on the day the speeches were to be given, neither had done any work on the project.

Chris dared Pat to say he'd been a tollbooth collector, and Pat dared Chris to say he'd toured with a circus. An hour later Chris told the class tales of traveling with a carnival, befriending the bearded lady, and having to bunk with the rubber-faced man. He never did admit he was making it all up as he went along.

Chris and Pat both wanted to become professional comedians, so they got themselves a gig at a tiny bar. They were to go on together just after midnight, but as usual they didn't bother to plan anything ahead of time. The bleary-eyed night shift workers in the audience were not amused. But the boys were thrilled to have made a start. They convinced themselves that one guy had looked as if he might have wanted to laugh, and they did their act again the following night.

Then the rest of the rugby guys heard what was going on, and the whole team said they were coming for the boys' third appearance. That night Chris and Pat chickened out, and their friends, who had paid a cover charge to see the show, were disgusted with them.

When the annual school variety show was announced, Chris and Pat agreed to be in it. They thought about doing a

They Died Too Young

spoof of *The Dating Game* and lined up two other guys and a girl to help. But the night of the show arrived, and they still hadn't planned anything. Then the girl dropped out, and the boys told each other they couldn't go on.

The event was so big that Pat and Chris could see the searchlights in the sky from their apartment. When they finally called the theater to say they weren't coming, the show was already in progress. The person who answered said, "Get over here! Now!" In the background about 2,000 voices could be heard chanting, "Farley, Finner, Farley, Finner."

Chris and the others drove over to the theater, scared to death. As they waited in the wings, Chris said, "Pick a character."

Pat said, "I'll be cool guy."

Another boy had overalls, so Chris said, "You be farm guy." He told the fourth boy, "You introduce us. I have glasses, so I'll be nerd guy."

Suddenly they were on, and the fourth guy made the introduction. Pat walked out doing his best to mock a cool guy. Next "farm guy" entered with a straw between his teeth and tipped his hat to the crowd. The audience loved it.

Then it was Chris's turn. He came out running full force, tripped over nothing, and slid almost the entire length of the stage. Then he jumped on a chair and tried about four or five ways to sit on it. The audience was going crazy, but the actors still had no plan and no actress.

Finally one of them announced, "We have no girl, but we do have a song." They sang *The Brady Bunch* TV show theme, and the huge audience sang along.

Chris and his friends were the hit of the show. When they got offstage, Chris grabbed Pat by the lapels of his shirt. Eyes sparkling, he panted, "We're gonna be doing this the rest of our lives." Those were prophetic words.

Chris guest stars as Chef Farley, with cast member
Kenan Thompson, on the Nickelodeon show *All That.*

LOOK OUT WORLD, HERE I COME

In his senior year, everyone at Marquette knew who Chris was, and people were beginning to believe that he might eventually become a professional comedian.

But Chris also had a serious side, and he dated one girl on a steady basis for a while. When she moved on, he found her hard to replace. Other girls were more likely to be grossed out than impressed by his rude noises and pratfalls.

Chris enjoyed the bar scene at Marquette and did plenty of partying. He loved to be around people and was famous for his version of "the naked beer slide," in which beer is poured on the floor and the "slider" strips down to the bare essentials. He then takes a run for it and throws himself on the floor to slide in the beer.

Life was good until Chris pulled a really dangerous stunt. One sunny spring day Chris decided to have some fun with the girls who lived in a big white house near the vacant lot where he and his buddies played baseball. He neglected to think about what could happen before he set a smoke bomb on the ledge of an open window of the girls' house and lit it.

Much to Chris's surprise, the smoke bomb spun around and fell into the house, setting fire to an old purple couch, the curtains, and the rug. When the fire department and the police cars began to arrive, he panicked and ran.

Dean Price learned that Chris had driven across the border into Illinois to hide, and he phoned the frightened Farley. Price told Chris that "at least no one was injured" and talked him into coming back. His shocked parents got him a lawyer.

Eventually Chris was found guilty of "dangerous use of firearms" and sentenced to do community service. His job was to read stories to little kids on playgrounds all over Milwaukee. Chris was wonderful at it. He treated his charges with great gentleness and told them his own extra-exciting versions of "Billy Goat Gruff" and other tales.

In the spring of 1986, Chris took part in graduation exercises at Marquette and returned to Madison to spend a year working at his father's paving company. He also tried stand-up comedy at a little club called Comedy Cellar. But Chris was a flop because he never planned out his act.

He soon moved on to the Ark Improvisational Theatre. There actors took suggestions from the audience and improvised scenes for the situations suggested. Chris became a huge favorite with the crowds because of the way he threw himself into his work.

A year later Pat Finn graduated from Marquette, and they headed for Chicago. Both hoped to get auditions at Second City, the mecca of improvisational humor. After all, they had been improvising their whole college careers.

Second City was where John Belushi got his big break and where Belushi had studied with the famed Del Close. After a brief career as an actor, Close became more famous as a teacher of theater arts. The theater company was started in 1959 by a group of University of Chicago students, since the school had no drama department. This experiment by amateurs was soon famous for training professional comedians.

In Chicago, Chris and Pat took odd jobs to pay the rent and hit the comedy clubs at night. "We'd get a job in a butcher shop," says Pat, "but we'd get fired for being too slow. Next day Chris would work at a hardware store, but he fell asleep on the boxes."

The boys wound up being on the stage at Improv Olympics every night and taking classes during the days. They often worked until four in the morning, and drinking was about the only vice they could afford.

After a year of being in a show almost every night, the boys finally had a night off. Chris moaned, "I can't believe we're not on stage tonight. You don't know what it's like for me to not be on the stage."

Finally, one night Del Close saw Chris being funny and liked what he saw. Close had been away from Second City for a while, but he had just been invited back. He insisted on bringing his own cast, including Chris Farley.

Working under Close, Chris learned that the best way to connect with his audience was to get to their souls. Rather than going for the easy joke, Chris was told to react with total honesty. Close believed that, in seeing someone else face their fears and weaknesses, the audience would identify with that character and the humor would be more personal and complete.

Chris was also forbidden to invent characters who were just stereotypes. Close wanted characters with quirks that made them different. He said he would rather see a comedian work though an idea to its logical conclusion, no matter how awkward, than stick with what was safe.

Comedians new to Second City always got sent out with touring companies, and it could take years before they ever performed on the main stage. Chris was only on the road a few months before he was brought back to Chicago. Although some performers complained that Chris hadn't paid his dues, most realized that he was ready.

Second City was a tough grind. They did two shows a night, six days a week, but Chris was fast becoming a true professional.

While Chris was at Second City he found a pair of old boots that he was sure his idol, John Belushi, had worn. Chris clomped around in those boots for the whole two years he was in Chicago.

Many of the characters that Chris invented on the Second City stage had problems that involved being fat. He was forever falling on things and breaking them, often bruising himself. But Pat remembers that one of Chris's funniest characters was different. He was a weatherman who

Steve Martin (left) shares a laugh with *Saturday Night Live*
producer Lorne Michaels (center) and Chevy Chase
during a press conference at the third annual
U.S. Comedy Arts Festival in Aspen, Colorado.

kept apologizing for the weather, saying things like, "There might be showers, and I'm really sorry. I'd like to say 10 percent, but I have to say 30 percent." It proved he could get laughs without being so physical.

One summer Chris met a writer named Bob Odenkirk from *Saturday Night Live*. Odenkirk had taken some time off from writing to get back into performing, and he had created a crazy character who was a motivational speaker. Gradually Odenkirk realized that Chris would be far better than he at doing this person, and Chris dubbed his new character "Matt Foley" after his old rugby coach.

Usually motivational speakers inspire people to reach their full potential by reciting glowing tales of success. The character Matt Foley, however, was a failure who lived "in a van down by the river." As he paced back and forth, hiking up the pants that kept sliding below his huge belly, he continuously adjusted his thick glasses and preached to the crowd. He told them they must succeed so they didn't turn out like he had.

Soon Lorne Michaels of *Saturday Night Live* was hearing glowing reports of a new comedy talent named Chris Farley. Michaels asked people at Second City about Chris and was told that the young comedian was great. But those who knew Chris also warned Michaels that Chris was fast becoming known for something besides his comedy. He seemed to have the same tendency to abuse alcohol and drugs that haunted Belushi.

Michaels flew Chris to New York to see *SNL* in person. Chris immediately knew that this was what he wanted and wanted badly. The two talked, and Michaels made it clear to Chris that, if *SNL* were even going to consider him for the show, he would have to stay off drugs and alcohol.

Coproducer Mike Shoemaker remembered, "We told him we didn't need another John Belushi." Belushi died of a drug overdose in 1982. Chris promised he would shape up.

John Belushi starred as Jake Blues in the 1980 Universal Pictures release *The Blues Brothers.*

Back in Chicago, Chris continued his improv at Second City and waited to hear from Michaels. Months went by and suddenly Michaels was in Chicago to see Chris in action. Unfortunately Chris wasn't in action. A few days earlier he had thrown himself into his portrayal of a toxically mad "Whale Boy" so enthusiastically that he'd broken his ankle.

More weeks went by, and in August of 1990, Michaels came to Chicago again. This time Chris was ready, and he put on a dynamite show. Michaels signed him up for *Saturday Night Live* the next morning.

The young fellow from the land of butter and cheese was on his way to the Big Apple. Again he was following in the steps of John Belushi and loving every minute of it.

The cast of *Saturday Night Live* poses on the show's set in
New York on September 22, 1992. In the front row, from
left, are Chris Farley, Al Franken, and Melanie Hutsell.
Middle row, from left, are Chris Rock, Julia Sweeney, Dana
Carvey, and Rob Schneider. In back row, from left, are
Adam Sandler, David Spade, Ellen Cleghorne, Kevin
Nealon, Phil Hartman, and Tim Meadows.

SATURDAY NIGHT LIVE

On September 12, 1990, a Madison newspaper proclaimed, "Hometown Boy Makes It Funny: Catch his name now, because beginning October 27, this Maple Bluff–raised comedian will be on his way to fame as a regular featured player on *Saturday Night Live*."

Even bigger than Chicago, New York was a very scary step for Chris. But *SNL* was also its own little world, almost like a high school with Lorne Michaels as principal. Chris and David Spade hung out together a lot and asked to share an office. Later they shared space with Chris Rock and Adam Sandler as well, all of them on the same humorous wavelength.

In short order Chris became one of the most popular performers on *SNL*. His character Matt Foley, the motivational speaker, became a regular, and sometimes Matt crept into Chris's other characters. For example, Chris's news correspondent Bennett Brauer had the same finger pointing way of making his case as Foley and shared his ability to live without showering.

Chris was called on to play people from many time periods and backgrounds. He imitated other comedians like Tom Arnold and Dom Deluise, and he pretended to be characters from the past, including Confucius and Jed Bowie, the imaginary rough-and-tough son of pioneer Jim Bowie.

Wearing a dozen different wigs, Chris played hysterically funny but not totally convincing women. A very funny sketch involved Adam Sandler singing a tribute to his school lunch lady while Chris, wearing a short, sack-like dress with a pinafore and sensible shoes, did an interpretive dance. No real-life lunch lady could have been more graceful or have kicked higher than Chris.

A high point of the 1993 season was his dead-on spoof of a hair-care infomercial that singer-actress Cher had done. In a long blond wig and a gorgeous gown, Lori Davis (played by Chris) told of her new hairspray that was "so exciting" her ditzy female viewers could hardly stand it. In fact, one swooned and had to be told to put her head between her legs.

Chris performed in ensemble sketches with the rest of the *SNL* cast, too, and one sketch was so popular that it returned for several installments. "Bob Swerski's Super Fans" revolved around four beer-swilling, nonstop eaters who met at a restaurant in Chicago each week to discuss their favorite teams: "Da Bearsss" and "Da Bullsss."

His Midwest background of football, basketball, and beer made Chris a natural for this group. His Milwaukee-Chicago accent was authentic, and being Irish himself, he *was* "Todd O'Conner."

The Super Fans were so devoted to the Chicago teams that their discussions were often about how badly "Da Bullsss" would beat the other guys. Todd once predicted a 402–0 score, adding, "Michael Jordan will be held to under 200 points." While they discussed such weighty matters, the guys feasted heartily on bratwurst, Polish sausage, knockwurst, pork chops, and cheese fries. As a result, poor Todd had frequent heart attacks. But he always managed to join his pals when they reversed their two-sided baseball caps from "Bears" to "Bulls."

Since *Saturday Night Live* had a new guest host each week, Chris had the chance to work with dozens of celebrities. In 1991 Michael Jordan himself appeared in an episode of "Super Fans." In 1992 Chris met the real Tom Arnold, and they became great friends. In 1993 Chris appeared as a very disturbed Santa Claus in a sketch with Sally Field; in 1994 he skated with Nancy Kerrigan; and there were many, many more.

But the character that best revealed Chris's own personality was the host of "The Chris Farley Show." Jim Downey, *SNL*'s producer, had noticed how Chris was awed by celebrities. When his heroes like Chevy Chase or Dan Aykroyd would come back to appear on the show, Chris would get all goofy and say things like, "Ah, do you remember when you . . . ?" The famous personality would answer yes, and the only thing Chris could then think to say was, "That was awesome."

Perhaps the funniest episode of this sketch was on February 13, 1993, when Chris, twitchy with excitement, interviewed former Beatle Paul McCartney. Paul assures the obviously nervous Chris, "You're doing fine," and that helps a little. Chris brings up various things Paul has done over the years, and Paul agrees that, yes, he did them. Then Chris asks Paul, "Do you remember that time there was a rumor you were dead?" Paul admits that the rumor did exist. Chris thinks hard and asks, "That was a hoax, right?"

Chris was always funny on Saturday night, but he was funny around *SNL*'s offices during the week too. For a while he went around with one eyebrow taped up high on his forehead so he'd look like John Belushi's mad pirate character. And just to make his friends laugh, he would purposely fall down hard, often hurting himself.

Everyone around NBC apparently loved Chris. "But he never did get away from that show-off thing," said coproducer Mike Shoemaker. "He was a gentle, sweet soul, who connected with people, but he had trouble talking to girls."

When Chris wasn't on stage, he might be found in church or working at a soup kitchen, a side of his personality that he kept very quiet. His small apartment in Lower Manhattan was filled with pictures of his family and paintings of sad-faced clowns.

As often as he could, Chris went back to Wisconsin and would show up at a grocery store, or a concert, or any kind of ball game in Milwaukee or Madison. He was a devoted fan of the Wisconsin University Badgers and even wrote a

SNL cast members Chris Farley and Dana Carvey share a laugh on the set of the NBC show during a news conference in New York, September 23, 1992.

sports column for his local paper in 1994. The guys at the Northgate Barber Shop in Madison saw Chris on a regular basis. The owner acknowledged that Chris could afford to get his hair cut anywhere, but when he was in town, he went to his old familiar barber. "He can talk to us."

If Chris loved any spot on earth more than Madison it was the Minoqua-Woodruff area of northern Wisconsin, where he'd gone as a Boy Scout. The tall trees and blue waters reminded him of a simpler time in his life.

Back in New York, Chris loved being on *SNL,* but there was one big problem: he wasn't onstage enough. All the

They Died Too Young

SNL players complained about that, but it especially upset Chris. Now that he had more money and more time, he spent even more time partying. Women he met at that time were often only interested in being seen with a celebrity. With his over-the-top, trusting personality, Chris consumed ever increasing amounts of food, alcohol, and drugs.

On at least two occasions Lorne Michaels had to inform Chris, "You have to leave the show and go into rehab." In 1992 Tom Arnold staged an intervention for his friend that some said kept Chris sober for three years.

Others aren't so sure Farley ever stopped abusing his body after he really got started. On one occasion when Chris was supposedly "on the wagon," Spade went to use Chris's phone and found beer cans everywhere and "weed laid out." Chris insisted the cans and the marijuana belonged to someone else. When Spade didn't buy it, Chris started crying and admitted, "I have a problem."

Then there was "The Fatty Arbuckle Incident," which the cast of *Saturday Night Live* teased Chris about for years afterward. But the allegations were anything but funny. Supposedly Chris started "coming on to" a female extra and wouldn't leave her alone when she complained. This incident got its name because, back in the 1920s, a famous overweight comedian named Fatty Arbuckle had ruined his career when he attended a wild party where a girl died.

Chris was also getting tired of always being "the fat guy who fell down." He wanted to move on, but it seemed the public wouldn't let him. Would he ever break free to show what he could really do?

David Spade played Richard Hayden and Chris was
Tommy Callahan in the film *Tommy Boy*.

BREAKING INTO MOVIES

Many of the cast members on *Saturday Night Live* moved on to movie careers. Chris was soon offered bit parts. In 1992 he played a security guard in *Wayne's World*. The following year, he played Milton the wanna-be roadie in *Wayne's World 2* and had a small part in *Coneheads*. He got more film exposure in Adam Sandler's movie *Billy Madison* in 1995.

Around the same time *Saturday Night Live* was taking tremendous criticism for being dead in the water. Chris felt the critics' jabs deeply. He later said, "We went out there and did an hour-and-a-half show every week and worked our [rears] off. . . . We were just trying to make people laugh, not do brain surgery. I've still got sores . . . and aches from going out a window . . . or landing on a coffee table. Let's see you guys try to make 20 million people a week laugh from a live comedy stage, 20 weeks a year."

Ready for bigger things, Chris signed a two-movie contract with Paramount Pictures. Lorne Michaels's idea for the first movie was to pair Chris with his exact opposite, David Spade, in a film to be called *Tommy Boy*. It was a formula that had worked for Laurel and Hardy, and it worked for Farley and Spade.

Of course it didn't hurt that in this movie Chris was really playing himself. His character, Tommy Callahan, has just graduated from Marquette University, the same college Chris went to. Tommy is expected to take over his father's business, again a situation Chris had lived through. Tommy even wears Chris's old rugby jacket from his days on the team. David plays a prim, businesslike person hired to keep Tommy from getting into trouble—a hopeless assignment.

The sweet, funny film fit Chris's bumbling but well-meaning personality perfectly. When Tommy first meets David's character, Richard, he says, "Lots of people go to college for seven years."

"Yeah," replies Richard, "they're called doctors."

Then Tommy tours his dad's auto parts factory and moves into his new office. He's constantly hurting himself and acting like a silly child, while Richard rolls his eyes in response.

Tommy's dad is about to marry a much younger beauty, who just happens to have a "son" about Tommy's age. Tommy is happy for his dad and delighted to finally have a brother. At the wedding, Tommy is having a great time when Dad has a heart attack and dies. Suddenly Callahan Auto Parts is in trouble. Determined to save the day, Tommy offers to go on the road to sell more auto parts. What results is a hilarious trek across the northern states in Richard's beloved blue convertible, which gets demolished. First, it loses a door when Tommy backs up at the gas station. Later, in probably the movie's funniest scene, a presumed-dead deer that the duo found on the highway and threw in the back seat suddenly comes to life and kicks the stuffing out of the car.

Tommy is a terrible salesman, but under Richard's coaching he gradually learns to get it right, and the company is eventually saved. But then it is revealed that Tommy's new "brother" is really the stepmother's lover, and they have been planning to fleece the company all along. The "brother" purposely confuses the shipping orders to all the customers, and Tommy's girlfriend is blamed.

When the stepmom and the "brother" go off to sell the company, Tommy and Richard must get to Chicago in a hurry to stop the deal. The guys can't get airline tickets, so they pose as airline attendants with riotous results, especially when Chris tries to change clothes in a tiny airplane restroom. Of course they save the day, and Chris even gets the girl.

Chris was proud of his movie and wanted desperately for everyone else to like it. But when *Tommy Boy* was released

Chris was the disaster-prone brother of a political candidate with David Spade as Steve Dodds, in the Paramount Pictures release *Black Sheep*.

in the spring of 1995, the critics tore it apart. Judy Nichols of the *Christian Science Monitor* called it a "mindless-entertainment flick" with "way too many gags" and a "thin plot with lots of rough edges."

The *Village Voice*'s Jeff Salmon complained, "*Tommy Boy* is the latest piece of sausage from the [*SNL*] factory, and since it was mostly ground out of Chris Farley's hide, the fat to meat ratio is even higher than usual."

Peter Travers of *Rolling Stone* wrote, "'He's a big, dumb animal,' says [David's character], nailing Tommy Boy as the sad freak show it is."

Other reviewers gave Chris some credit for being funny. An *Entertainment Weekly* article by Chris Nashawaty stated, "Farley's Baby Huey-as-frat boy shtick can be a hoot. . . . Granted this is no *Blues Brothers,* but the boys riff off each other hilariously."

Entertainment Weekly's Owen Gleiberman said, "In *Tommy Boy,* [Farley] keeps getting plonked in the face by large, heavy objects. There's nothing very funny about the gag—until you get to Farley's reaction, which is so angry, so naked in its God-I-can't-believe-I-did-that-again self-hatred, that I chuckled every time."

Chris, a sensitive guy at heart, was crushed by the negative reviews. He continued to drown his misery in the usual way: food, booze, drugs, and, since this was show business, women.

But then his fans—mostly young men of high school and college age—were heard from. In its first week out, *Tommy Boy* took in $8,000,000, number one for all movies released that week. In its second week it took in $16,300,000. *Tommy Boy* continued to rate high with moviegoers, and in late October it became one of the top 10 moneymakers in video rentals too. A year later the film had grossed $32,700,000. It even earned Chris and David an MTV award for best on-screen duo.

The public had spoken, and studio executives listened. Suddenly Chris and David were being offered all kinds of scripts. Warner Bros. wanted Chris to do *The Cable Guy,* and Chris loved the script. He figured he could do it between projects for Paramount, but Paramount informed him he was still under contract for a second movie, and he was going to make *Black Sheep* right away. Warner Bros. couldn't wait two years for Chris, so they went with Jim Carrey.

Chris did enjoy being a star. That April he was invited to Washington, D.C., to spoof Newt Gingrich, then Speaker of the House of Representatives. In a white wig, Chris looked exactly like Gingrich and had a ball convincing the House Judiciary Committee to push through a bill declaring all Democrats officially weird and to have the nation's capital moved to Atlanta.

To promote *Tommy Boy* Chris appeared on the late night shows with Jay Leno, Conan O'Brien, and David Letterman.

Chris impersonates House Speaker Newt Gingrich on Capitol Hill, April 4, 1995.

On *The Tonight Show,* Chris appeared as "Mayor Cheddar McFarley." Joining Letterman onstage, Chris did cartwheels, fell off a chair, and pretended to have a heart attack.

When he wasn't hobnobbing with celebrities, Chris often did charity appearances for his church, his former schools, his hometown, or complete strangers. When fans asked him for an autograph, Chris couldn't do enough for them.

Unfortunately Chris was also a regular at wild parties and sometimes had to be carried home. His friends could see he was getting out of control. They urged him to take it easy. Chris knew he should slow down the crazy merry-go-round his life had become, but he just couldn't do it.

Chris Farley and David Spade in *Black Sheep.*

GROWING CAREER, GROWING PROBLEM

With *Tommy Boy* quickly becoming a cult classic, Chris went to work on *Black Sheep,* his second movie with David Spade. The plot was very similar to that of *Tommy Boy.* This time Chris plays Mike Donnelley, whose brother is running for governor of Washington State. Again Chris's character is huge, well-meaning, and constantly hurting himself and embarrassing those around him. Again David Spade's character is called in for damage control.

The movie opens with Mike driving around in a sound truck encouraging everyone to vote for his brother. Distracted by a pack of dogs following the truck, Mike clips off a whole row of parking meters and comes to a stop only when his truck wedges itself under a movie marquee. He's embarrassed his brother.

The conniving woman governor running for reelection against Mike's brother sees possibilities here and orders her flunkies to get Mike in really hot water. Her cronies get Mike fired from his job at the local rec center and try to get him blamed for setting the rec center on fire. But before that can happen, Mike is sent off to hide out at a remote hunting cabin. David Spade's character goes along to keep track of the troublemaker.

The cabin is in bad shape and gets lots worse once our heroes arrive. Soon they are sleeping in the rain with a missing roof and fighting over who gets the top bunk. Mike, still wanting to help his brother's campaign, manages to staple his finger to a tree and roll down a very long hill. The guys also tangle with a local survivalist who has some interesting relatives.

Finally the lady governor comes up with a picture of Mike running from the burning rec center and gets it published in all the papers. She wins the election, and it looks as if all is lost.

But Mike begins to wonder about the voter numbers he's hearing. The county where he and Spade's character have been hiding out has cast more votes than they have registered voters. The boys break into some county offices and learn that the survivalist's long-dead relatives voted in this election.

Another desperate car chase is in order (more shades of *Tommy Boy*), part of it in a borrowed police car. Mike arrives in the nick of time to save the day for his brother.

Chris enjoyed making *Black Sheep* and got his brothers John and Kevin bit parts as security guards so they could all hang out together.

Although the critics hated *Black Sheep* even more than *Tommy Boy*, they couldn't argue with its $10,600,000 take on its first weekend out. Some studio types even began to compare Farley and Spade to comedy greats like Laurel and Hardy. Penelope Spheeris, *Black Sheep*'s director, told *Entertainment Weekly,* "When I was growing up, there were Martin & Lewis and Abbott & Costello. This generation hasn't seen this kind of thing. But people just love to see these guys having a good time."

Chris and David, though, refused to get trapped in the Laurel and Hardy mold. After working together so closely for so long, they admitted they were getting on each other's nerves. They needed to separate and explore other possibilities.

Columbia Pictures offered Chris a martial arts comedy called *Beverly Hills Ninja*. He would finally get to use his body for things besides falling down and running into heavy objects. To prepare for his role, Chris studied at the Championship Marital Arts Academy in Chicago for three months, where he learned "wu shu," a method that uses both hand-to-hand combat and weapons like the three-section staff, broadsword, nunchaku, and chain. Chris was good at wu shu and enjoyed the challenge. He also got to wear

Chris arrives for the Los Angeles premiere of his film *Beverly Hills Ninja*.

some far-out clothes in the movie, and his costar was a gorgeous blond named Nicollette Sheridan.

Unfortunately, the plot was just another variation of the bumbling, well-meaning idiot trying to prove himself. He had an on-screen baby-sitter in this picture, too, but instead of David Spade it was a real Japanese ninja.

In one of the film's funniest scenes, Chris gets caught by the airport metal detector because he's carrying enough swords and fighting gear in his underwear to fill a huge trunk. Another scene has him doing a half-naked dance with some strippers, and another has him pretending to be a Japanese chef who can't handle his cutlery.

Beverly Hills Ninja made another bundle of money, and again Chris made a triumphant tour of the talk shows. But like Chris's other two movies, it also got terrible reviews. *Entertainment Weekly* said, "Stop this guy before he makes *Goat Boy: The Movie.* [Grade:] D + ."

And critics weren't the only ones trying to stop Chris in those days. Everyone he knew, including Lorne Michaels, David Spade, Dan Aykroyd, Tom Arnold, his manager, and of course, his family, begged him to cut back on his wild living and to get his weight under control. Directors were getting leery of hiring Chris for fear he would self-destruct before their movies could be finished. He was sent off time and time again to fat farms and detox centers.

When Chris got lectures on his behavior, he always agreed that he needed to improve, but he also acted as if it were some kind of a game. He bragged about how Tom Arnold helped him escape from a weight control center in Santa Monica and how they then ate "tons of desserts." He compared himself to Jackie Gleason, who would slim down only when he lost the ability to do cartwheels and pratfalls.

Chris's older brother Tom was frustrated with Hollywood's attitude toward drugs and excessive partying. He told *Rolling Stone,* "Every time I read something in the paper, it's like . . . 'It's good for his career, so he's got to lose some weight.' . . . When is someone going to be concerned about his well-being? . . . I'd rather have a live bum than a dead ex-star."

Chris insisted that he wanted to be a good Catholic but that he was powerless over his personal demons. He said he wanted to settle down with a nice girl and have children. It worried him that this might never happen.

Month after month Chris fought his cravings for food, alcohol, drugs, and sex. Some said he was going the final mile in his obsessive quest to relive Belushi's life. They pointed out that Belushi had died of a drug overdose at 33, and Chris was fast approaching that age. Others believed that Chris was actually afraid to lose weight. They thought that maybe he was thinking people only watched him because they liked to see "the fat boy fall down."

But a fan who met Chris on the beach while the comic was filming *Black Sheep* probably put his finger on the real problem. Seeking to pay Chris the ultimate compliment, the fan said, "If you like how he acts you will like him even more in person, he is absolutely the same." In other words, Chris was always "on." He was caught in a terrible trap that was partly of his own making. He'd been playing the outrageous party-guy moron for so long he couldn't stop. On-screen or off, he felt he had to be the person his fans expected.

"No one can be 'on' 100% of the time," Del Close warned him. "Human beings aren't 1,000 watt fuses; we're 15 watt fuses, and we blow."

They Died Too Young

Chris was almost ready to blow when he finished his last starring role in a movie. During the filming of *Almost Heroes* in the fall of 1996, Chris was forced to attend Alchoholics Anonymous meetings daily. When he did a voice-over for Dream Works, a real-life, full-time baby-sitter was assigned to him, the role David Spade had played on-screen.

Almost Heroes concerns two explorers out to beat Lewis and Clark to the Pacific. Chris, as Bartholomew Hunt, is another fat, bumbling guy playing against the thinner, more sophisticated Edwards (Matthew Perry). Perhaps the best thing about this flick, from Chris's point of view, was that for once he got to play the smarter guy. In fact, it's Edwards who falls off a wagon in one of the opening scenes, and it's also Edwards who makes most of the terrible choices in this movie.

One of the funniest parts of the movie is when Hunt needs to find an eagle's egg so that an Indian woman can make a potion to cure Edwards's fever. Chris must walk miles through the snows of the Rocky Mountains just to find the nest at the top of a very tall pine. He climbs up and up, and suddenly the eagle attacks, hurtling him to ground. Although he succeeds in keeping the egg from breaking, he's also starving. Unable to stop himself, he cooks the precious egg and eats it. He must return to the top of the pine, and again the eagle attacks. He eats the second egg too, then goes after the third and final one. Again the eagle attacks, but this time, after much difficulty, Chris gets the egg back safely to the Indian woman. She immediately smashes the egg and informs Chris that all she needed was the shell.

Chris was then paid $6 million a picture. He played a cameo role in *Dirty Work* and was slated to do a movie called *The Gelfin*. He was considering many others, and he talked endlessly about starring in Fatty Arbuckle's life story.

But it was not to be. Chris would die before he could do another movie.

Presenter Chris Farley hugs Best Animated Short Film
winners Tyron Montgomery (left) and Thomas Stellmach
(right) at the 69th Annual Academy Awards in
Los Angeles, March 24, 1997.

THE FINAL ACT

The stage was set for disaster. At an *SNL* cast reunion in Aspen in March 1997, Chris was heavier than ever and sweating buckets. His friends were very worried about what might happen to him.

In August he got kicked out of a Malibu rehab clinic for disruptive behavior. "He was obsessed with Belushi," said his drug counselor. "Chris thought he needed to be loaded to excess in order to be accepted."

The following month *Us* magazine ran an article entitled "Chris Farley: On the Edge of Disaster." Writer Erik Hedegaard wondered if Chris would live long enough to fulfill his dream of playing Fatty Arbuckle. It would have been his first chance at a serious role.

On October 25, 1997, in a *Saturday Night Live* tradition, Chris was slated to return as guest host. He arrived direct from a rehab center, and although he was supposed to have a chaperone, he was alone and already bombed. The entire week was one big party, according to one source.

Lorne Michaels and the staff of *SNL* agonized over whether to let Chris do the show. Michaels was later criticized for his decision, but it was a tough call. Michaels explained, "I think it was enormously important to Chris that he host the show. There was no question that he was in trouble, but the thing that made Chris Farley beautiful was that he was funny, and how do you deny that to someone who is a performer?"

The show's first sketch was too close to the truth for comfort. Tim Meadows is trying to convince Michaels that Chris is fit to be guest host. Michaels asks Meadows how he can be sure that Chris won't screw up, and suddenly Chris bursts into the room. "Because I won't!" he shouts. Then he brings out his "sponsor" from AA in the form of Chevy Chase, known for his own substance abuse problems. Meadows concludes, "Fatty falls down, ratings go up."

Other sketches had Farley playing a shy Catholic schoolboy, his Matt Foley character, and Hank Williams Jr., who is recording a *Monday Night Football* song. As usual, Chris put everything thing he had into his work. At times it appeared he could barely breathe, and there were rumors that oxygen tanks waited in the wings just in case he needed them.

The reviews were mixed, but one said, "An instant classic. . . . It was the funniest [*SNL*] show in a long time. . . . Farley's overall presence gives the show [an] . . . A + ."

After that Chris went back to rehab for a few weeks and then home to Chicago for Thanksgiving. He told his friend Jillian Seely, a reformed alcoholic, that the *SNL* gig had been a nightmare for him. He began drinking more heavily than ever. Jillian tried hard, but she couldn't help Chris. "I know he wanted to get sober," she told *Rolling Stone.* "But it was like he had cancer and the chemo treatment didn't work any more."

In December Chris was back at Hazelden, a rehab center in Minnesota he'd visited so often a friend claimed they should name a wing after him. He spent just one night there, returning to Chicago on December 11. Over the next few days, he went to Mass, baked Christmas cookies, bought a pretrimmed Christmas tree, and talked with Jillian about *Almost Heroes* and the potential Fatty Arbuckle movie. He even went to an AA meeting.

But a few days later Chris began a final binge of epic proportions. He partied into the night at a club called Karma, where he joked about having a heart attack and passed out $50 tips. Then he went back to his condo to freebase cocaine.

The next day, Monday, he showed up at a party at Second City, where he seemed normal enough. Later that night, however, Dennis Rodman, the Chicago Bulls star with his own problems, met Chris at a nightclub and had one of his bodyguards take the comic home.

On Tuesday Chris hired an exotic dancer to entertain him at his condo. On Wednesday he hired another dancer to be with him while he drank vodka and consumed cocaine and heroin. He was passed out on the floor when the dancer left at 3:00 A.M. on Thursday.

It was on Thursday afternoon around 2:00 P.M. (December 18) that his brother John discovered Chris's lifeless body. Chris was lying on his back in his pajamas with a bloody liquid coming from his nose and white froth coming from his mouth. The fluid and froth immediately made the experts suspect the death was drug related, although Chris had been known to have high blood pressure. Some wondered if he'd finally had the heart attack he had pretended to have so many times before.

On Friday, Cook County's medical examiner announced that death was due to "opiate and cocaine intoxication" with "severe narrowing of the coronary arteries as a significant contributing condition." The opiate was heroin breaking down to morphine in the body. The doctors explained that the drug levels in Chris's body weren't outrageously high, but his veins were so clogged he should have had a heart bypass. "When you have a heart like he did," said one doctor, "it doesn't take a lot to push you over."

Memorial services for Chris were held in Chicago, New York, and Los Angeles, but the funeral itself was in his hometown of Madison, Wisconsin. At Queen of Peace Catholic Church, his family and friends—including Michael Price, Pat Finn, and his old Boy Scout leader—heard Father Foley (the real Matt Foley) give a magnificent eulogy. Security guards were there, too, protecting celebrities like Chris Rock, Dan Aykroyd, Adam Sandler, Tom Arnold, and Lorne Michaels from reporters and the curious.

David Spade was not there. When asked about that, Spade explained that he'd been devastated by the death of a close friend when he was 21, and he just couldn't stand to see Chris "in a box."

The following prayer was one that Chris carried in his wallet for years. It appeared on the back of a program handed out at his funeral:

A CLOWN'S PRAYER
As I stumble through this life,
help me to create more laughter than tears,
dispense more happiness than gloom
spread more cheer than despair.

Never let me become so indifferent
that I fail to see the wonder in the eyes of a child,
or the twinkle in the eyes of the aged.

Never let me forget that my total effort is to
cheer people, make them happy, and to forget, at
least momentarily, all the unhappiness in their lives.

And in my final moment,
may I hear You whisper,
"When you made my people smile,
You made me smile."

Chris's last movie, *Almost Heroes,* was released in 1998, after his death. Most of his family went to a private screening at Planet Hollywood in Los Angeles, but for the people who loved him, there were more tears than laughs.

His parents vowed to use Chris's death to warn others that drugs can be fatal. They gave permission to Rebos House (a group of nonprofit rehab centers) to use Chris's picture on hundreds of billboards and posters to be put up in schools. A new branch of Rebos House was later named after him.

The posters showed a smiling Chris Farley, and under the image were the words "Drugs and Alcohol Can Kill the Laughter in Anybody."

They Died Too Young

Further Reading

Arnold, Roseanne. *My Lives*. New York: Ballantine, 1994.

Cader, Michael, ed. *Saturday Night Live: The First 20 Years*. Boston: Houghton Mifflin, 1994.

Hedegaard, Erik. "Chris Farley, 1954–1997." *Rolling Stone*, February 5, 1998, pp. 39–46.

———. "Chris Farley: On the Edge of Disaster." *Us*, September 1997, p. 103.

Nashwaty, Chris. "The Last Temptation of Chris." *Entertainment Weekly*, January 9, 1998, pp. 22–27.

Tresniowski, Alex, and Giovanna Breu. "Requiem for a Heavyweight." *People*, January 12, 1998, pp. 47–50.

Chronology

1964	Chris Farley is born in Madison, Wisconsin, on February 15.
1982	Graduates from high school.
1986	Graduates from Marquette University; works at father's paving business for a year; also works at Comedy Cellar and Ark Improv.
1987	Moves to Chicago.
1988	Meets Del Close and is hired at Second City.
1990	Meets Lorne Michaels and is hired by *SNL*; Chippendale skit airs on October 27.
1992	Appears in a bit part in *Wayne's World*; Tom Arnold tries to get Chris get off drugs.
1993	Has small roles in *Wayne's World 2* and *Coneheads*.
1994	Appears in *Airheads*.
1995	Appears in *Billy Madison*; stars in *Tommy Boy*; impersonates Newt Gingrich in Washington, D.C.
1996	Stars in *Black Sheep*.
1997	Stars in *Beverly Hills Ninja*; films a bit part in *Dirty Work*; guest hosts *SNL*; is found dead on December 18.
1998	*Almost Heroes*, his last movie, is posthumously released.

Filmography

Movies

Wayne's World, 1992

Wayne's World 2, 1993

Coneheads, 1993

Airheads, 1994

Billy Madison, 1995 (unbilled cameo)

Tommy Boy, 1995

Black Sheep, 1996

Beverly Hills Ninja, 1997

Almost Heroes, 1998

Dirty Work, 1998 (cameo)

Television

The Jackie Thomas Show, 1992

The Larry Sanders Show, 1993–94

Tom, 1994

All That, 1995

Dennis Miller Live, 1995

MTV's "Road Rules," 1996

MTV's Black Sheep Promo, 1996

The Tonight Show, 1997
  (as Mayor Cheddar McFarley)

INDEX